Little Wandle Handwriting

8

Handwriting

Workbook 8

Joining letters

Rachel Davis MBE and Manreet Ratan

Unit 1: Diagonal joins from the baseline to short letters

k

Write the letter.

k k k k k k k k k k

Write the unjoined word.

kick kick

Letter check-up

k k

ki kn

Draw the pattern.

Write the letters.

ki ki

kn kn

Letter join check-up

ki

kn

Unit 1: Diagonal joins from the baseline to short letters

im in

Draw the pattern.

Write the joined letters.

im im

in in

Letter join check-up

in

im

Write the words.

Kim Kim

Fin Fin

Additional practice

Jim Jim

kin kin

Word check-up

Unit 1: Diagonal joins from the baseline to short letters

am ar

Draw the pattern.

Write the joined letters.

am am

ar ar

Letter join check-up

am

ar

Write the words.

yam yam

jar jar

Additional practice

jam jam

bar bar

Word check-up

Unit 1: Diagonal joins from the baseline to short letters

ur ir

Draw the pattern.

Write the joined letters.

ur ur

ir ir

Letter join check-up

ur

ir

Write the sentence.

Our jam in a jar.

Additional practice

Sir Tim in a bin.

Word check-up

Unit 1: Diagonal joins from the baseline to short letters

um un

Draw the pattern.

Write the joined letters.

um um

un un

Letter join check-up

um

un

Write the words.

gum gum

bun bun

Additional practice

yum yum

pun pun

Word check-up

Unit 1: Diagonal joins from the baseline to short letters

ti tu

Draw the pattern.

Write the joined letters.

ti ti

tu tu

Letter join check-up

ti

tu

Write the sentence.

I tip in a bun.

Additional practice

Gum in a tin.

Word check-up

Unit 1: Diagonal joins from the baseline to short letters

li lu

Practise making your letter joins smooth.

Draw the pattern.

lililili lililili lililili lililili

Write the joined letters.

li li

lu lu

Letter join check-up

li

lu

Write the words.

plum plum

lip lip

Additional practice

limp limp

plump plump

Word check-up

Unit 1: Diagonal joins from the baseline to short letters

hi di

Draw the pattern.

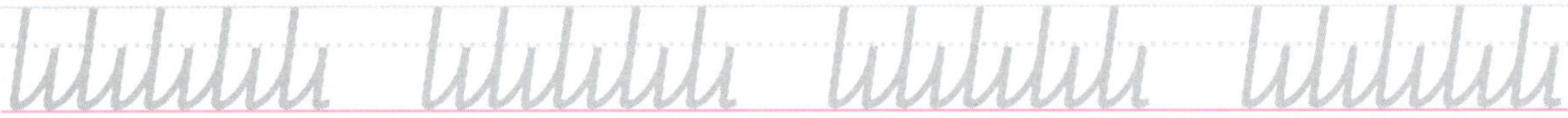

Write the joined letters.

hi hi

di di

Letter join check-up

hi

di

Write the sentence.

A glum hippo in a dip.

Additional practice

A plum in a tin.

Word check-up

Unit 1: Diagonal joins from the baseline to short letters

he ie

Draw the pattern.

eeeee eeeee eeeee eeeee

Write the joined letters.

he he

ie ie

Letter join check-up

he

ie

Write the words.

hen hen

pie pie

Additional practice

hey hey

lie lie

Word check-up

Unit 1: Diagonal joins from the baseline to short letters

en ee

Draw the pattern.

eeeee eeeee eeeee eeeee

Write the joined letters.

en en

ee ee

Letter join check-up

en

ee

Write the sentence.

See a hen in a tie.

Additional practice

Sheep lie in a pen.

Word check-up

Unit 1: Diagonal joins from the baseline to short letters

su se

Draw the pattern.

sısısısı sısısısı sısısısı sısısısı

Write the joined letters.

su su

se se

Letter join check-up

su

se

Write the words.

sun sun

seem seem

Additional practice

sum sum

sew sew

Word check-up

Unit 1: Diagonal joins from the baseline to short letters

es ss

Draw the pattern.

sssss sssss sssss sssss

Write the joined letters.

es es

ss ss

Letter join check-up

es

ss

Write the sentence.

When Sam misses me he hisses.

Additional practice

Jess guesses in a game.

Word check-up

Unit 2: Diagonal joins from the baseline to tall letters

sh th

Draw the pattern.

ddd ddd ddd ddd

Write the joined letters.

sh sh

th th

Letter join check-up

sh

th

Write the words.

ship ship

think think

Additional practice

dish dish

bath bath

Word check-up

Unit 2: Diagonal joins from the baseline to tall letters

ch cl

Draw the pattern.

clclcl clclcl clclcl clclcl

Write the joined letters.

ch ch

cl cl

Letter join check-up

ch

cl

Write the sentence.

The sheep cluster in the pen.

Additional practice

Ashley bathes her chimp.

Word check-up

Unit 2: Diagonal joins from the baseline to tall letters

sl st

Draw the pattern.

Write the joined letters.

sl sl

st st

Letter join check-up

sl

st

Write the words.

sleep sleep

nest nest

Additional practice

slipper slipper

stump stump

Word check-up

Unit 2: Diagonal joins from the baseline to tall letters

nt et

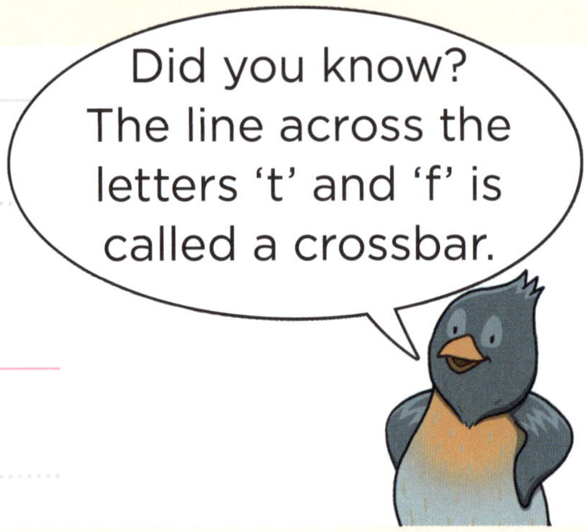

Draw the pattern.

Write the joined letters.

nt nt

et et

Letter join check-up

nt

et

Write the sentence.

I get the best sleep in my tent.

Additional practice

Janet steps in slimy paint.

Word check-up

Unit 2: Diagonal joins from the baseline to tall letters

al at

Draw the pattern.

ulul ulul ulul ulul

Write the joined letters.

al al

at at

Letter join check-up

al

at

Write the words.

palm palm

bat bat

Additional practice

gale gale

pats pats

Word check-up

Unit 2: Diagonal joins from the baseline to tall letters

ut ub

Go 'up the iceberg' for a smooth diagonal join.

Draw the pattern.

ulul u ulul u ulul u ulul u

Write the joined letters.

ut ut

ub ub

Letter join check-up

ut

ub

Write the sentence.

Nate put lip balm in a tub.

Additional practice

Caleb the cute cub slept by

the gate.

Word check-up

ll tt

Draw the pattern.

llll llll llll llll

Write the joined letters.

ll ll

tt tt

Letter join check-up

ll

tt

Write the words.

pull pull

mitt mitt

Additional practice

shell shell

kitten kitten

Word check-up

Unit 2: Diagonal joins from the baseline to tall letters

if it

Draw the pattern.

Write the joined letters.

if if

it it

Letter join check-up

if

it

Write the sentence.

Jill likes a little sleep if she is ill.

Additional practice

Fill the butter dish if it is empty.

Word check-up

ca ma

Draw the pattern.

aaaa aaaa aaaa aaaa

Write the joined letters.

ca ca

ma ma

Letter join check-up

ca

ma

Write the words.

canal canal

mast mast

Additional practice

camel camel

mail mail

Word check-up

Unit 3: Diagonal joins from the baseline to curly letters

ed ad

Draw the pattern.

aaaa aaaa aaaa aaaa

Write the joined letters.

ed ed

ad ad

Letter join check-up

ed

ad

Write the sentence.

Oscar made a red car.

Additional practice

The masked man had a black

cat.

Word check-up

Unit 3: Diagonal joins from the baseline to curly letters

ag ig

Draw the pattern.

Write the joined letters.

ag ag

ig ig

Letter join check-up

ag

ig

Write the words.

tag tag

big big

Additional practice

bags bags

digger digger

Word check-up

ac uc

Draw the pattern.

Write the joined letters.

ac ac

uc uc

Letter join check-up

ac

uc

Write the sentence.

The big duck quacks again.

Additional practice

My backpack had a zig zag tag.

Word check-up

Unit 3: Diagonal joins from the baseline to curly letters

do to

Draw the pattern.

ccccc ccccc ccccc ccccc

Write the joined letters.

do do

to to

Letter join check-up

do

to

Write the words.

dots dots

into into

Additional practice

undo undo

auto auto

Word check-up

Unit 3: Diagonal joins from the baseline to curly letters

iq eq

Draw the pattern.

ccccc ccccc ccccc ccccc

Write the joined letters.

iq iq

eq eq

Letter join check-up

iq

eq

Write the sentence.

Please do cut the cake into

equal slices.

Additional practice

Put the liquid into a cup.

Word check-up

Unit 4: Horizontal joins from the mid-line to short letters

oi or

Draw the pattern.

Write the joined letters.

oi oi

or or

Letter join check-up

oi

or

Write the words.

coil coil

torn torn

Additional practice

spoil spoil

corner corner

Word check-up

ow on

Draw the pattern.

ovovov ovovov ovovov

Write the joined letters.

ow ow

on on

Letter join check-up

ow

on

Write the sentence.

Lorna the spoilt lion has a shiny crown.

Additional practice

Boil the yellow corn on the stove.

Word check-up

ou oe

Draw the pattern.

ouou ouou ouou ouou

Write the joined letters.

ou ou

oe oe

Letter join check-up

ou

oe

Write the words.

pour pour

goes goes

Additional practice

touch touch

shoe shoe

Word check-up

Unit 4: Horizontal joins from the mid-line to short letters

ri ru

Draw the pattern.

rrrrr rrrrr rrrrr rrrrr

Write the joined letters.

ri ri

ru ru

Letter join check-up

ri

ru

Write the sentence.

The clown tried to run in his

silly shoes.

Additional practice

Brian goes out to play rugby

in his slippers.

Word check-up

Unit 4: Horizontal joins from the mid-line to short letters

we wi

Draw the pattern.

eveve eveve eveve eveve

Write the joined letters.

we we

wi wi

Letter join check-up

we

wi

Write the words.

went went

winter winter

Additional practice

weather weather

swims swims

Word check-up

Unit 4: Horizontal joins from the mid-line to short letters

fe fr

Draw the pattern.

Write the joined letters.

fe fe

fr fr

Letter join check-up

fe

fr

Write the sentence.

The wise fruit bat ate fewer insects.

Additional practice

I went to a festival with my friends.

Word check-up

Unit 5: Horizontal joins from the mid-line to tall letters

ol ot

Draw the pattern.

Write the joined letters.

ol ol

ot ot

Letter join check-up

ol

ot

Write the words.

hole hole

spot spot

Additional practice

bolt bolt

robot robot

Word check-up

Unit 5: Horizontal joins from the mid-line to tall letters

rh wh

Draw the pattern.

rlrlrlrl rlrlrlrl rlrlrlrl rlrlrlrl

Write the joined letters.

rh rh

wh wh

Letter join check-up

rh

wh

Write the sentence.

Colin the white rhino dances on the spot.

Additional practice

I eat rhubarb crumble whether it is hot or cold.

Word check-up

Unit 5: Horizontal joins from the mid-line to tall letters

ff ft

Draw the pattern.

ololol ololol ololol ololol

Write the joined letters.

ff ff

ft ft

Letter join check-up

ff

ft

Write the words.

puff puff

gift gift

Additional practice

cliff cliff

drift drift

Word check-up

Unit 5: Horizontal joins from the mid-line to tall letters

fl wl

Draw the pattern.

ololol ololol ololol ololol

Write the joined letters.

fl fl

wl wl

Letter join check-up

fl

wl

Write the sentence.

The owl flew over the soft

fluffy rabbit.

Additional practice

My sister often makes me

tasty waffles.

Word check-up

Unit 6: Horizontal joins from the mid-line to curly letters

ra wa

Draw the pattern.

rororo rororo rororo rororo

Write the joined letters.

ra ra

wa wa

Letter join check-up

ra

wa

Write the words.

raven raven

water water

Additional practice

frame frame

warmer warmer

Word check-up

Unit 6: Horizontal joins from the mid-line to curly letters

oa va

Draw the pattern.

cococ cococ cococ cococ

Write the joined letters.

oa oa

va va

Letter join check-up

oa

va

Write the sentence.

The van was racing down the road.

Additional practice

The goat ran away across the vast field.

Word check-up

Unit 6: Horizontal joins from the mid-line to curly letters

od rd

Draw the pattern.

oaoao oaoao oaoao oaoao

Write the joined letters.

od od

rd rd

Letter join check-up

od

rd

Write the words.

body body

card card

Additional practice

today today

pardon pardon

Word check-up

Unit 6: Horizontal joins from the mid-line to curly letters

og rg

Draw the pattern.

oaoao oaoao oaoao oaoao

Write the joined letters.

og og

rg rg

Letter join check-up

og

rg

Write the sentence.

The guard dog charged at the

rodent.

Additional practice

The large frog heard an odd

sound from the tree.

Word check-up

Unit 6: Horizontal joins from the mid-line to curly letters

oc rc

Draw the pattern.

rrrrr rrrrr rrrrr rrrrr

Write the joined letters.

oc oc

rc rc

Letter join check-up

oc

rc

Write the words.

sock sock

torch torch

Additional practice

cocoa cocoa

marches marches

Word check-up

Unit 6: Horizontal joins from the mid-line to curly letters

fo oo

Draw the pattern.

ooooo ooooo ooooo ooooo

Write the joined letters.

fo fo

oo oo

Letter join check-up

fo

oo

Write the sentence.

I purchased food at the local shop.

Additional practice

I searched for my grey school socks.

Word check-up

Practice

Practice

William Collins' dream of knowledge for all began with the publication of his first book in 1819.
A self-educated mill worker, he not only enriched millions of lives, but also founded a flourishing publishing house.
Today, staying true to this spirit, Collins books are packed with inspiration, innovation and practical expertise.
They place you at the centre of a world of possibility and give you exactly what you need to explore it.

Published by Collins
An imprint of HarperCollins*Publishers*
The News Building, 1 London Bridge Street, London, SE1 9GF, UK

HarperCollins*Publishers*
Macken House, 39/40 Mayor Street Upper, Dublin 1, D01 C9W8, Ireland

Browse the complete Collins catalogue at
collins.co.uk

Created in collaboration with Wandle Learning Trust.
www.littlewandle.org.uk

10 9 8 7 6 5 4 3 2 1

A catalogue record for this publication is available from the British Library.

ISBN 978-0-00-885340-2

Authors: Rachel Davis and Manreet Ratan
Publisher: Laura White
Product manager: Caroline Green
Product developer: Julianna Dunn
Copyeditor: Sarah Snashall
Proofreader: Sally Byford
Font designer: Jamie Clarke
Penguin illustrations: Noah Warnes
All other illustrations: Joseph Wilkins (Beehive Illustration)
Cover designer: Kneath Associates
Internal designer: David Jimenez
Typesetter: 2Hoots Publishing Services Ltd
Production controller: Sophie Waeland

Printed and bound in the UK using 100% Renewable Electricity at Martins the Printers Ltd

Wandle Learning Trust and Little Sutton Primary School have partnered with HarperCollins*Publishers* to provide teachers with a full systematic synthetic phonics programme, Little Wandle Letters and Sounds Revised, and accompanying Collins Big Cat readers. Full details of the programme, including CPD training, can be found at www.littlewandlelettersandsounds.org.uk.